DR. TERRANCE STONE

HOW TO MOVE IN A ROOM FULL OF VULTURES

HOW TO MOVE IN A ROOM FULL OF VULTURES

Introduction

How to Move in a Room Full of Vultures: A Memoir of Redemption and Leadership

Some rooms weren't built for you to win in. Some were built to watch you fail, to study your downfall, to celebrate your silence. I've stood in those rooms: boardrooms, classrooms, trap houses, courtrooms, and I've felt the weight of expectation that I wouldn't survive any of them.

But I did.

I wasn't born with privilege. I wasn't handed opportunity. I was born into pain, into poverty, into a world where survival was the first lesson and silence was survival's twin. I learned to move young; through chaos, through violence, through grief. And somewhere in that storm, I found my voice.

This book isn't about glorifying the streets. It's not about bragging rights. This is about the lessons that nearly broke me and the redemption that rebuilt me.

How to Move in a Room Full of Vultures is a roadmap written in scars. It's a testament to what happens when you stop letting the room define you and start defining the room. When leadership isn't about position, it's about presence. When your story becomes your strength instead of your shame.

You'll read about a boy who lost his father too early, got swallowed by the system, baptized in gang culture, and hardened by prison walls, but who refused to let that be the final chapter.

You'll also read about a man who returned to those same streets not to conquer, but to serve. A man who founded *Young Visionaries Youth Leadership Academy* not because it was easy, but because it was necessary. Because I knew there were kids out there like me angry, brilliant, unseen and they didn't need another lecture. They needed a lighthouse.

This is not just my story. It's a mirror for every young person trying to outrun their past, and a manual for every leader who's ever felt alone at the table. It's proof that your mess doesn't disqualify your mission. And it's a call to anyone moving through rooms where vultures circle: *keep your head up, your heart clear, and your purpose loud.*

Because redemption is real. And leadership ain't about being the loudest, it's about being the light.

Welcome to my story. But more importantly, welcome to yours.

— *Dr. Terrance L. Stone*

Acknowledgments

First, I want to thank God - for mercy, for redemption, and for the vision to see beyond my circumstances.

To my mother Susan, for her resilience, her love, and her unwavering belief in me even when I didn't believe in myself.

To my family – my kids, all my brothers and sisters who were there for the journey, through the pain and the progress.

To the youth I've had the privilege of mentoring - you're the reason I keep going. Your courage, your questions, and your potential fuel my purpose.

To every educator, probation officer, counselor, mentor, and ally who supported Young Visionaries - you believed in what we stood for before the world could see it.
To my community and every block that shaped me. I am you. This book is for you.

To the homies who didn't make it - your stories are in these pages. Your names stay on my heart.

And finally, to the vultures - thank you. You taught me how to move with purpose, how to lead with presence, and how to rise without losing my soul.

This isn't just my story - it's our testimony.

Disclaimer

The stories, events, and characters depicted in this book are based on real-life experiences, observations, and reflections but some names, details, and timelines may have been altered or dramatized for storytelling purposes. Certain parts might be entirely factual, while others may blend memory, perspective, or creative license.

This book is not meant to glorify crime, trauma, or street life. Its purpose is to uplift, inspire, and empower people, especially youth, to realize their potential, make positive choices, and embrace transformation.

The ultimate message is this: **no matter where you come from, you can rise above your circumstances and become something greater.**

This story is a testimony, not a blueprint and the heart behind it is one of healing, growth, and hope.

Table of Contents

PART I: SURVIVING THE STORM

CHAPTER

1

WE WERE JUST KIDS

South Central Los Angeles. I was two years old, small and barely speaking, yet already absorbing the language of the streets the rhythm of cars, the crackle of static from old radios, the lingo exchanged between men with afros and gold chains. His hand felt warm and strong, wrapping around my tiny fingers, pulling me safely across the street. I still remember the texture of his palm calloused, but comforting. Cars cruised by, bass thumping to The Dramatics' "What You See Is What You Get." The sun was shining. Palm trees swayed overhead like they were watching over us. And to me, he was a giant black leather shoes that clicked against the concrete, bell-bottom pants that flared like wings, and a butterfly collar shirt that seemed to scream confidence.

A voice called out from across the street, "What's up, young blood?"

My father grinned, that wide, toothy smile only he had. "What they hit fo'?" he said, pulling out a wad of cash and a pair of dice from his pocket. The dice clicked in his hand like bones. He knelt beside me, held out the dice. "Blow on these for good luck, son."

That would be the last time I saw my father alive.

A week later, I saw him again but this time, he was center stage in a church, lying still inside a casket. A silk suit replaced the wild shirt. His hands folded neatly over his chest. He had overdosed on heroin. Dumped like garbage on a sidewalk. Needle still in his arm. Left by so-called friends too high to help.

That was the day I learned what loss felt like. Real loss. The kind that doesn't knock, it breaks the door down. My mom held me tight while my older brother Marcus and sister Michelle sat beside us. We were a strange mix of siblings' same father, different mothers, stitched together by grief. That day we gathered, not for a birthday or a reunion, but for a "homegoing." That's what Black folks call it when we say goodbye with love and dignity, even when the end was ugly.

After that, we left the Jordan Downs Projects in Watts. My grandmother, aunts, and Uncle Tim all packed up and followed us to 2222 Academy Street in Pomona, California. A new city, but the same storm. We weren't escaping anything, we were just rerouting it, like a river that always finds its way back to the ocean.

Pomona was different, but not better. The violence wore a different outfit, but the pain felt the same. I started noticing the patterns early single moms grinding double shifts, young men disappearing into the system, the slow hum of police sirens like a lullaby you never wanted to fall asleep to. It was like living inside a song that never reached its chorus just the same loop of struggle over and over again.

We were poor, but I didn't really understand what poverty was until I started seeing how other people lived. We had roaches. We had eviction notices. We had late-night arguments and early morning knockdowns. I learned young how to sleep through gunshots and how to tell the difference between fireworks and a .38.

My mom, Susan, was everything. Factory jobs, long hours, and a spine made of steel. She didn't use drugs, didn't drink, didn't complain. What I inherited from her wasn't just blood, it was that relentless hustle. That iron-willed persistence. But even strong women have soft spots. Hers was for tough guys. Street dudes with game and scars. And that weakness? That attraction? It would end up putting more weight on all our backs.

The days were long, and the nights were longer. Sometimes, when the streetlights came on, we weren't rushing home. We were watching fights in the parking lot, sneaking into abandoned vans, or staring down older kids who already carried pieces in their waistbands. Violence wasn't something that shocked us, it was something we rehearsed.

That first experience of loss changed me. I didn't know it then, but it hardened something inside. Not just pain but pressure. And pressure creates one of two things: cracks or diamonds. For a long time, I lived in the crack. I started understanding what power looked like in my world who got respected, who got stepped on, and who didn't make it out. And I made a silent promise to myself: I would never be one of the ones stepped on again.

Chapter One Notes

Quote: "It's not where you start, it's where you decide to go next."

Lesson: Even in the darkest beginnings, seeds of strength are planted.

Leadership Takeaway: Real leaders are shaped by struggle.

Reflection Prompt: What moment in your early life forced you to grow up faster than you should have

CHAPTER

2

THE COLONIALS

Pomona was supposed to be a fresh start, but it quickly became just a different chapter in the same book. When we moved into The Colonials, an apartment complex on the west side of town it felt like stepping into a new kind of jungle. One with cracked concrete instead of grass, broken swings instead of trees, and the sound of arguments replacing birdsong.

The Colonials had a rhythm. You learned to move to it fast. Early morning doors slamming as parents rushed to low-paying jobs, the laughter of unsupervised kids echoing through breezeways, and the deep thump of basslines vibrating from cars with stolen speakers. Everything in those apartments breathed energy, chaos, and survival.

I met Toriano there. My stepfather's son. We were just five months apart, but it felt like we had a lifetime of difference between us at first. He was light-skinned, curly-haired, quick-tempered. I was dark-skinned, quiet, stubborn. We looked nothing alike, but soon enough, we were inseparable. School, fights, food, even clothes we shared it all. We were two little boys figuring out how to become men in a world where boys didn't get the luxury of softness.

When my stepfather brought Toriano to live with us, it wasn't like he asked. One day he showed up, and suddenly there was another kid in my room, touching my toys, sleeping in my space. I was supposed to be cool with it. But I wasn't. At least not at first.

Fighting became part of our language. We scrapped over everything, TV time, food, attention. But in that scrapping, something deeper formed: brotherhood. Not the fake kind. The real kind that's forged through pain and proximity.

The adults in our lives were deep in the street life. My step-father Bill, people called him Cool Bill or Steel Bill, was one of the founding members of local the Crips Gang we grew up in and around. Before that, he was a part of the Businessmen, a street crew from back when Black men wore suits but still carried steel. He and his brothers were respected. Feared. They carried themselves like kings in a crumbling kingdom.

When they were around, the rules changed. We kids weren't just playing anymore, we were proving something. One day, they were drinking in the front room while me, Toriano, and our younger brother Jarron were in the back arguing. Toriano started pushing me. Teasing me. Testing me.
I'd had enough.

I reached into my back pocket and pulled out my cake cutter comb long steel teeth and a black power fist on the handle. The kind you used to pick out an afro, but that day, I used it as a weapon. I swung. Stabbed him right in the arm. Blood came quick. Our uncles came running but not to break it up. They laughed. One of them slapped me on the back.
"Lil man got heart," he said.

That day, I learned something twisted and dangerous: violence wasn't just a reaction it was a tool. A performance. And when done right, it earned you respect. That became a script I'd follow for years.

But the Colonials weren't just about blood and beatdowns. They were also home. I remember jumping fences to swim in the pool after hours, begging for candy at the corner unit, throwing rocks over the freeway wall, and running from angry neighbors. It was wild, but it was ours.

We had our own economy, our own rules, our own entertainment. The local drug addict named Mike used to get high on PCP and scare the kids. They'd lock him in an old abandoned van, and we'd circle around it, waiting to see if he'd bust out like some horror movie monster. It was insane but to us, it was Saturday night.

Even in chaos, we had community. If your mama ran out of sugar, you could knock on any door. If you got into a fight, someone's older brother would step in before things got too serious. We didn't have much but we had each other.

And yet, under it all, there was this slow-building pressure. Like the walls were closing in, even if you didn't see them move. Kids were getting older. Tougher. Angrier. The games were turning serious. And I could feel it in my gut: something big was coming. Something dark.

The Colonials were never just a place we lived. They were the proving ground. The first battlefield. And every kid who grew up there came out either broken or bulletproof.

Chapter Two Notes:

Quote: "Brotherhood isn't always born it's built in the fire of shared survival."

Lesson: Even in conflict, there's connection.

Leadership Takeaway: Real leaders don't avoid tension they use it to build trust.

Reflection Prompt: Think of someone who challenged you. How did it shape your strength?

CHAPTER
3

CRACKS IN THE PAVEMENT

I was thirteen when the real fracture happened. My mom, tired of being disrespected and abused, finally walked away from my stepfather. She packed her things and moved to Walnut a quiet, clean suburb where the grass got watered, and kids rode bikes in the street without fear.

But I didn't follow her. I couldn't. I wasn't ready to leave the noise behind. I wasn't ready to trade in chaos for calm. My friends, my crew, my neighborhood that was my identity. I stayed behind with my stepdad, not because he was good to me, but because the streets saw me. And even if they didn't love me, they acknowledged me. That mattered more than safety at the time.

The mid-1980s brought a storm one wrapped in little plastic baggies and served hot over homemade pipes. Crack cocaine was more than a drug, it was a culture shift. It turned boys into bosses and blocks into battlegrounds. Fast money. Flashy cars. Fearless attitudes. We went from asking our moms for lunch money to having more cash than grown men. We didn't save. We didn't plan. We just flexed.

I remember the first time I felt rich. Not real rich, but hood rich. I had just come up on a bundle, and my pockets were heavy. I bought a Porsche 944 from a smoker. No license. No insurance. It didn't matter. I was sliding through the city in a stick-shift car I could barely drive. I didn't even know what an oil change was. That car died fast. So, I copped a Cadillac and repeated the cycle.

Everything was about appearance. Fila suits, Sergio Tacchini tracksuits, shell toes laced just right. We had no idea how deep we were sinking. We were too busy floating on a false sense of freedom. We'd hit Crenshaw, music blasting, girls in the passenger seat, windows down living like every day was the first verse of a rap video.

But the police saw it too.

We got pulled over constantly. Especially in my boy Curtis's white Nissan truck. Curtis had a real dad in his life one who made sure the car was legit. Registration, insurance, clean title. That truck was legal. So, when we got pulled over in it, the cops couldn't impound it. They hated that. I remember sitting on the curb while they tore through the vehicle, hoping to find something to justify their harassment. They never did. We had stash boxes. Hidden compartments. Practice.

One day, I was just chilling in the complex. Wasn't even slinging. I had about a thousand dollars in my pocket, just because. I was wearing corduroys, a Fila shirt, and my Mets jacket feeling myself. I had my pager on my hip like it was a Rolex. A group of younger dudes were around me, eyes wide, soaking it all up. I pulled out my stack of money, showed it off like it was a trophy. Then I saw him.

Sheriff Robinson. Short dude, always angry, with a mean streak you could feel before he even opened his mouth. He walked through the complex gate with some lady beside him. I tucked my money back in my pocket quick, but it was too late. He saw.

He lined us up. Searched the first guy. Skipped me. Searched the next. Then came back to me.

I remembered what my Uncle Butch had told me: "They can't search you without a warrant. Don't let them punk you."

So, when Robinson reached for my pocket, I slapped his hand away.

That's all it took.

He snapped. Pulled out his baton and started swinging like I was some wild animal. Blow after blow. I screamed, "Help! Help!" but nobody moved. I tried to run, but he tackled me. Pinned me. And then, he pulled a gun from his ankle holster and pointed it at my head.

I swear, if no one had been watching, if neighbors hadn't peeked out their windows, I might not be here. Instead, I got arrested. Charged with attempted murder of a police officer. They claimed I reached for his weapon.

He showed up to court in a neck brace like he'd just survived a plane crash. I didn't even land a punch.

The judge gave me sixteen years. California Youth Authority. I was just a teenager.

But the streets had taught me one thing: show no weakness. So, I didn't cry. I didn't beg. I took the sentence like a soldier. On the outside, I was tough. On the inside, I was scared.

Scared of what was next. Scared of losing more of myself.

Chapter Three Notes:

Quote: "Fast money comes with slow consequences."

Lesson: What feels like freedom can quickly become your cage.

Leadership Takeaway: Discipline is harder than hustle—but it lasts longer.

Reflection Prompt: When did you realize a fast choice came with a slow consequence?

CHAPTER

4

GLADIATOR SCHOOL

CYA - California Youth Authority. It sounded like some kind of training camp for leaders or politicians. But for those of us sentenced there, it was a warzone disguised as rehabilitation. We called it Gladiator School.

It was the survival of the fittest. Not just physically, but mentally, emotionally. If you didn't figure out how to protect your mind, your soul, your peace, you were going to lose it all. Some guys went in with dreams and came out broken. Some never made it out at all.

When I got off that bus, shackled and staring at the gates of my new home, I remember thinking, "This is where boys die or become monsters."

It wasn't just the inmates who made it hard. The guards were part of the system too. Some were cool, some were cruel. And the ones who were cruel enjoyed showing you who held the keys. Every meal, every phone call, every letter from the outside was a privilege, not a right. They reminded you of that.

My first cellmate was a kid named Reese from Long Beach. Short, stocky, tattooed up even at 17. We didn't talk much at first. Just observed. That's what prison does, it turns conversation into calculation. But eventually, we started exchanging stories. And what I learned shocked me. Different city. Same struggle. We were all just kids playing grown men's games.

The first fight I saw wasn't mine, but it shook me. Two guys going at it over a phone. One took a tray to the face. Blood hit the wall like a horror movie. Nobody stepped in. The guards just let it happen. Lesson learned: don't ask for help. Handle your business.

I started working out daily. Push-ups. Sit-ups. Anything to keep my body ready. But I also trained my mind. I read books, autobiographies, street novels, anything I could get my hands on. I started to think beyond the block, beyond the walls. I didn't know it yet, but the first seeds of transformation were being planted.

Still, that change wasn't instant. I was still angry. Still hard. Still ready to fight at any moment. And I did fight. More than once. Each fight was like a performance. You didn't just win you sent a message: "Don't test me."

Time passed slowly in CYA. Letters from home became lifelines. When my mother wrote, I read her words like scripture. Her handwriting reminded me that someone still believed in me. It kept a small piece of my humanity alive.

There was a guy there named Eric, older than most of us, close to aging out. One night during lockdown, he leaned over from his bunk and said, "You ever think about what comes after this?"

I didn't answer. But I thought about it all night. What *did* come after this? Would I go back to the same streets? Same habits? Or was there something more? Something better?

By the time I was released at nineteen, I had the muscles, the rep, and the walk of someone who'd seen hell and made it back. But I was still lost. I didn't know how to be free because I had never really been free in the first place.

And I didn't last four months.

I went right back to the life.

I didn't go back weak. I went back *worse*. I was "certified" now. That meant something in the streets. People respected me. Or feared me. Sometimes both. That was power or so I thought.

Chapter Four Notes:

Quote: "You don't grow through what you go through you grow when you reflect on it."

Lesson: Pain without reflection just hardens you. Reflection builds resilience.

Leadership Takeaway: Leaders are forged in fire but healed through truth.

Reflection Prompt: What pain have you been through that you haven't fully reflected on yet?

CHAPTER

5

THE STREETS KEEP CALLING

F reedom didn't feel like freedom.

When I walked out of CYA at nineteen, the sun felt different on my skin. Brighter. But also artificial. Like a spotlight on a stage, I wasn't ready to perform on. I was back in the world but I was still caged inside. My mind hadn't caught up to the release date printed on my paperwork.

The streets welcomed me back like I never left. Word spread quick Terrance's home. Homies pulled up. Fists turned to hugs. We celebrated like it was a victory, but deep down, I didn't know what I had won.

I bought a '77 blue Cadillac Seville. That car wasn't just transportation, it was a chariot. A throne on wheels. I'd roll with my boys, music thumping, windows down, bouncing through the city like kings returning to a conquered land. That Seville became a symbol. When people saw it, they knew who it was.

We weren't just riding. We were staking territory. Sliding through neighborhoods like we were bulletproof. And most days, we acted like we were. Reckless. Loud. Armed. Ready.

We had routines. We'd circle the block. Post up on the corner. Size up anyone unfamiliar. Sometimes it was just about presence showing that we still ran the streets. Other times, it was more direct. Confrontation. Intimidation. Escalation.

I was respected now. But what I didn't realize was that respect rooted in fear is really just quiet rejection. Nobody really wants to love a monster they just don't want to get bitten.

That car carried us to countless memories. Some still haunt me. Others that made us laugh until we couldn't breathe. I remember one night pulling into the parking lot of a liquor store. The energy was tense. Someone had disrespected one of our people earlier that week. We didn't go looking for peace. We went looking for payback.

A few words. A few gestures. Then it popped off. Bottles thrown. Guns pulled. We peeled out of that lot with screeching tires and pounding hearts. I remember gripping the steering wheel so tight my knuckles turned white. That night could've been the end. But somehow, we made it out. We always did. Until the one day we wouldn't.

But we didn't think that way back then. Death wasn't a fear it was an expectation. We were young Black men living on borrowed time. The question wasn't "if" it was "when."

Some nights I'd park the Seville and just sit in silence. The engine ticking as it cooled. My thoughts racing faster than I ever could on foot. I'd wonder, "Is this it?" This loop of violence, street fame, fast money, and faster enemies? I felt trapped. But I didn't know any other way to live.

And then there were the kids.

Little dudes watching us from behind bikes and front porches. Studying us like we were gods. Mimicking the way we stood, the way we dressed. I saw myself in their eyes, and for the first time, it scared me. Because I knew exactly where their path led.

It wasn't that I didn't want change. I just didn't know how to find it. I had the scars. I had the name. I had the experience. But I didn't yet have the vision. That would come later. For now, I was just surviving. And surviving ain't living.

Chapter 5 Notes:

Quote: "Your reputation can open doors or dig graves."

Lesson: What feels like respect on the block may cost you your future.

Leadership Takeaway: Real leadership ain't about fear it's about influence.

Reflection Prompt: What image were you trying to live up to that no longer serves you?

PART II: HITTING ROCK BOTTOM

CHAPTER

6

THE SETUP

Trouble doesn't knock twice when it knows the door's always open. Mine wasn't just open, it was wide with a welcome mat.

The setup didn't come from strangers. It rarely does. It came from someone I thought I could trust someone from the inside. Someone who wore the same colors and spoke the same code. That's what hurt the most. Not the charge. Not the time. But the betrayal.

We were supposed to be brothers. But out here, desperation will make people sell their own blood. And in our world, you didn't need a contract to seal your fate just a whisper in the right ear.

I was living fast, reckless, trying to make a name out of scars. And I did. But I made enemies too. Enemies in blue. Enemies in rival hoods. Enemies that smiled in my face and wrote statements behind my back.

This one day, it all came down.

I was set up. Simple as that. A deal that was never real. A location that was too perfect. A silence that should've been loud. And I walked right into it confident, cocky, blind.

The arrest wasn't loud. No chase. No dramatic takedown. Just a cold "Turn around" and the click of steel on my wrists. The officers weren't even excited. It was like they'd already won. Like they'd been watching a movie and just waited for the credits to roll.

That's when it hit me.

You think the streets owe you something. You think because you've put in work, because you've taken hits and handed out pain, that there's some kind of loyalty. But there's not. There's just silence. Empty promises. And shadows.

Back in the system again, I wasn't surprised. I wasn't scared either. That's what made it worse. I had become numb. Desensitized. The bars weren't new. The routine wasn't new. It was like coming back to a house you didn't want to live in, but already had furniture in every room.

In that cell, though, I started thinking different. Not soft. Not scared. Just different. I started watching the young ones coming in 17, 18, barely old enough to grow facial hair. Some still with baby fat on their cheeks, talking tough like they'd been through wars. I saw myself in them. But I also saw where they'd end up.

One of the youngest guys, name was Devon, asked me, "You ever think we deserve better?"

I laughed at first. Then I thought about it. Not "better" like a mansion or a Benz. But better like peace. Like freedom from looking over your shoulder every second. Like waking up without plotting your next hustle.

That night, I wrote my first journal entry.
It was short. Sloppy. But real:
"I'm tired of fighting ghosts. Tired of proving I belong in a place I don't want to die in."

That one sentence didn't change my life overnight. But it cracked something open.
And from that crack, the light started leaking in.

Chapter Six Notes:

Quote: "Loyalty built on fear is the first step toward betrayal."

Lesson: Trust earned in the dark will be tested in the light.

Leadership Takeaway: Real leadership begins when you recognize the setup—and refuse to keep walking into it.

Reflection Prompt: Who in your life taught you the hardest lesson about trust? How did it change you?

CHAPTER

7

ON THE RUN AGAIN

They say paranoia will destroy you. But in my world, paranoia was just preparation. After that setup, after I saw how easy it was for people to flip, I stayed ready. Not just ready for war but ready to run.

The streets knew me. My name rang bells, but not all bells are praises. Some are warnings. I became both a target and a trophy. Some wanted me gone. Others wanted to be me. Either way, I couldn't sleep easy.

I was ducking warrants, ducking rivals, ducking trust. I had burner phones and backup plans. Stashed clothes in three different spots. My life became a series of exits. I stopped looking out of windows I started looking *through* them. Every noise outside made my heart jump. Every knock at the door felt like a final warning.

There was one week I didn't even go home. I stayed in motels. Ate fast food. I slept with one eye open. I rotated motels like outfits, paying in cash, and moving quiet. That was the week I realized something: freedom and fear often ride in the same car. And I was always in the driver's seat, too tired to keep going, too scared to pull over.

I wasn't just on the run from the law I was running from myself. From the guilt. From the pain. From the memories I refused to unpack. The truth is, you can lie to everyone around you, but you can't lie to the mirror. And when you've lived that life long enough, even your reflection looks like a stranger.

One night, I found myself in a cheap motel in San Bernardino. The kind with buzzing neon lights and cigarette burns in the carpet. I had a pistol on the nightstand and a pocket full of cash. The silence was deafening. I stared at myself in the mirror above the sink eyes hollow, soul quiet. And for the first time, I didn't recognize who I saw. Not just physically I had changed inside. The light in my eyes? Gone. I wasn't Terrance anymore. I was a ghost in my own story.

And ghosts don't build legacies. They haunt them.

I thought about everything that had happened up until that point. The fights. The betrayal. The homies who were gone. Some dead, some locked up forever. We used to say we were soldiers. But what army buries this many of its own?

That night, I didn't cry. I didn't scream. I just sat on the edge of the bed, listening to the hum of the fridge and the distant sound of traffic. My gun was within reach, and so was the thought: "Would anybody even care if I didn't wake up tomorrow?"

I knew I needed a way out. But I didn't know where to go. Who to call. I had burned more bridges than I could count. Some with gasoline. Some with dynamite. But deep inside, buried under all the pride and pain, was a whisper.

"You can still change."

It was faint. Easy to ignore. But it didn't leave. It followed me. It didn't shout it waited. And slowly, I started listening.

That moment didn't fix everything. I still had a long way to go. But that whisper planted a seed. One I would later water with purpose, pain, and prayer. That night, I made a silent vow: if I ever got another chance, I'd stop running from everything, especially myself.

Chapter Seven Notes:

Quote: "The longer you run from your past, the heavier your future becomes."

Lesson: You can't outrun what you won't face.

Leadership Takeaway: Leaders don't just confront threats they confront *themselves*.

Reflection Prompt: What part of yourself have you been running from, and what would it look like to face it?

CHAPTER

8

SIGNS FROM THE INSIDE

Prison walls don't just keep you in, they block everything out. The noise of the world fades behind concrete and steel, and all that's left is your mind, your past, and the choices that led you there. And sometimes, if you're lucky or maybe if you're just finally listening something bigger breaks through.

I started noticing signs. Not the kind written on paper or flashing on screens. These were spiritual signs. Unspoken warnings. Quiet confirmations. Subtle nudges from God or the universe or maybe just my own soul finally speaking up.

One came in the form of a simple moment. I was sitting on my bunk, eyes locked on a book I'd read three times already, but I wasn't really reading. My mind was stuck on replay, cycling through scenes of violence, betrayal, and everything I had become. Then out of nowhere, a CO walked past, stopped, looked at me, and said, "You ever think maybe you're supposed to be doing something different with your life?"

He didn't wait for an answer. He just kept walking like he hadn't dropped a spiritual bomb in my lap. But his words stuck. I tried to shake it off, "Man, he don't know me." But I couldn't let it go. Because deep down, I *had* been thinking that. And I was tired of acting like I wasn't.

Later that night, I got a slip under my cell door. No name. No handwriting I recognized. Just a verse from Proverbs: *"As iron sharpens iron, so one man sharpens another."* At the time, I didn't even fully understand it. But it hit different. It felt like a reminder. Like someone or something was telling me I wasn't made to rust in here. I was meant to be sharpened.

Then came the letter from my mom. A single line: *"Don't let this be the end of your story."* She didn't write more. She didn't need to. That one line told me everything. That she still believed in me. That she hadn't given up. And that meant I couldn't either.

Another day, a young dude in the next cell asked me for help writing a letter to his daughter. He was barely literate. Told me he didn't want her thinking he didn't care he just didn't know how to say the words right. That moment humbled me. I sat at my desk, pen in hand, and helped this kid write a message of love to a child he may not ever get to hold again. And while I was writing his words, I started hearing my own.

That's when I started to feel it purpose. Something deeper than respect. Something real. I wasn't born to be a lost cause. I wasn't born just to survive or get stripes. I had a voice. And that voice could do more than start fights or spit game it could lead.

So, I picked up a pen, not to write lyrics, but to write truth. I started journaling. About my past. My thoughts. My pain. I wrote about all the brothers I lost. All the nights I couldn't sleep. All the questions I had for God. Those pages became my mirror, and in them, I didn't just see who I was I started to see who I could be.

Maybe everything I went through wasn't punishment. Maybe it was preparation. A fire meant to burn away what I wasn't so I could step into what I was meant to be.

For the first time, I saw a future that didn't end in a box. Not a cell. Not a casket. But a calling.

The signs had been there. But it took stillness to see them. It took silence to finally hear what I had been drowning out for years.

That was the beginning of the shift.

Chapter Eight Notes:

Q **uote:** "Sometimes silence is the loudest message you'll ever hear."

Lesson: When everything around you goes quiet, listen for what's trying to rise from within.

Leadership Takeaway: Leaders are born not when they speak the loudest, but when they listen the deepest.

Reflection Prompt: What quiet moment in your life felt like a turning point—and did you listen to it?

CHAPTER

9

THE DAY ROOM AND THE DREAM

The day room was loud. TVs blaring, dominos slamming, trash talk flying back and forth like bullets. It smelled like sweat, stale chips, and cheap soap. It wasn't a place built for dreaming. It was a cage with corners to survive in. But somehow, in the middle of all that chaos, something broke through something that would change everything.

I was sitting against the wall, tuning most of the noise out, just sketching in a notepad I had traded for ramen. Some guys were playing chess nearby. Others were locked in a heated argument over a basketball game that happened three nights ago. Just another normal day in the belly of the beast.

Then I saw a kid young, maybe 17, get up in front of the TV and start talking. Loud. Passionate. Not angry, though. Not posturing. Just... *real.*

He said, "Y'all ever wonder what it would look like if we all came together? Like for real? No sets, no politics. Just us, as men. What would it look like if we turned this energy into something that builds instead of breaks?"

People laughed at him. Some booed. One dude threw a balled-up piece of paper. But I watched. I listened. And my heart started pounding. Because for the first time, someone said out loud the very thing I had only dared to write down.

What *would* it look like?

That night, back in my cell, I couldn't sleep. I kept hearing his words over and over. I thought about all the power we had inside us, wasted on war. We had skills hustle, strategy, leadership but no vision. What if we flipped the script?

I started writing again, only this time, it wasn't just about the past. It was about the future. I wrote out what a youth center might look like run by men who had survived the worst but came back to guide the next generation. I imagined us walking into schools, not with fear, but with respect. Suits instead of flags. Blueprints instead of beef.

It felt crazy. Wild. But it also felt like the first real dream I'd ever had that didn't involve money or revenge.

The day room became my think tank. Every spare moment, I wrote. Plans. Program ideas. Names of people I wanted to talk to. I even sketched a logo. I didn't know how or when, but I knew this vision couldn't die in a cell.

That dream became the seed for something much bigger.

It would later be called the Young Visionaries Youth Leadership Academy.
But before it had a name, it had a purpose.

And it was born in the middle of noise, chaos, and a room full of broken men trying to remember what it meant to be whole.

Chapter 9 Notes:

Quote: "Your vision doesn't need permission to be born it just needs belief to grow."

Lesson: The dream is possible, even if your surroundings look impossible.

Leadership Takeaway: Vision is the first step. Action is the second. Consistency is what makes it real.

Reflection Prompt: Have you ever had a dream that felt bigger than your circumstances? What would happen if you started planning for it anyway?

CHAPTER

10

PLANTING THE SEED

The dream had a heartbeat now. It wasn't just an idea scribbled in a notebook or a vision whispered in a jailhouse day room. It was alive. It was pulsing inside me, louder than the noise around me, stronger than the weight of my past. But to make it real, I had to plant it and protect it.

Most people think change happens in a flash of lightning. A big moment. A viral video. A second chance handed out like candy. But real change? It's slow. It's painful. It's planting a seed in rocky soil and showing up every day to water it even when nothing breaks through.

When I got out, I didn't come home to applause. I didn't come back with sponsors or support. I came back with an idea, a notepad, and the fire to make something out of the fire I came through.

I hit the streets again but not like before. This time, I wasn't out to be seen. I was out to *see*. I walked those same blocks with new eyes. I talked to the youth standing on corners where I used to post. I met them in barbershops, community centers, and sometimes outside courthouses before they went inside and got swallowed by a system I knew too well.

I realized quickly these kids didn't need more rules. They needed *reasons*. They needed someone who wasn't afraid of their pain. Someone who'd walked their walk and survived it. Someone who could look them in the eye and say, "I get it. But let me show you what comes next."

That was my lane. My calling.

I started showing up at churches, small-town rec centers, juvenile halls. No fancy suit. No letters behind my name. Just raw truth and a voice that couldn't be ignored. I told my story not to glorify the streets, but to show what redemption looked like in real time.

Some people didn't want to hear it. Doors got closed. Eyes rolled. I was labeled: ex-con, gangbanger, "trying too hard to be a savior." But I kept showing up. Even when it was just three kids in a folding chair. Even when the mic didn't work and the lights were too dim. I showed up. And that consistency started to build trust.

I called it Young Visionaries Youth Leadership Academy. It didn't have a building yet. It didn't even have a logo at first. But it had a pulse. A mission. A sacred fire to inspire the young, the lost, and the overlooked to lead with power and purpose.

I stayed broke those early years. Real broke. There were nights I skipped meals to keep the lights on at our little office space. I did odd jobs, spoke for free, and hustled legally just to keep the vision alive. But I never let go of it. And I never stopped believing that something bigger was coming.

I remember walking into a classroom one day and seeing a group of middle schoolers throwing paper, yelling, checked out. The teacher looked defeated. I stood there, took off my hat, and just said, "How many of y'all know someone locked up?"

Almost every hand went up.
Then I asked, "How many of y'all think *you're next?*"
The silence was loud.

That's when I knew: this work wasn't just needed. It was *urgent.*

There was this one kid named Jaylen. Fifteen. Angry. Loud. Dismissed by everyone. I saw myself in him. I pulled him aside one day and said, "You think you're tough 'cause you've been through pain. But real toughness is what you do *after* the pain."

He looked me dead in the eye and said, "Then show me."

So, I did.

I mentored him. Showed him structure. Held him accountable. I didn't coddle him. I challenged him. And he kept coming back. Week after week. Eventually, he started helping out setting up chairs, greeting new kids. Now? Jaylen's a mentor. A leader. A walking testimony that seeds really *do* grow when you give them time, truth, and love.

That's what planting the seed does. It doesn't just grow you grow *with it.*

And even when it rains, even when the ground is hard, even when no one else believes it grows.

Chapter 10 Notes:

Quote: "A dream planted in truth will grow even in broken soil."

Lesson: You don't need perfect conditions to begin. You just need to start.

Leadership Takeaway: Great leaders don't wait for support they build it from the ground up.

Reflection Prompt: What seed of change are you carrying right now and what's stopping you from planting it?

PART III: BECOMING THE LIGHT

CHAPTER

11

A NEW HUSTLE

Building Young Visionaries wasn't just about helping others it was about saving myself. The transformation I was going through wasn't pretty. It wasn't clean or smooth. It was messy. Hard. Lonely at times. But it is necessary.

See, I had spent years perfecting the street hustle. I knew how to flip a bag, dodge a case, and keep my name alive in the alleys and whispers. But this hustle? This new one? It was different. It was slow. It came with rejection, paperwork, and long nights full of doubt.

Nobody teaches you how to lead when you used to lead with fists. Nobody gives you a playbook for purpose when your past is a rap sheet. I had to unlearn everything that once kept me alive so I could become the man who helped others *live*.

Some days I questioned myself. Wondered if I was really built for this. I'd sit alone, surrounded by papers, grant applications, lesson plans, trying to speak life into something that felt like it might collapse at any moment.

But every time I felt like quitting, I thought about the kids.

Kids like Jaylen. Kids who looked at me not like a former gang member, but like proof that change was possible. They didn't need me to be perfect. They needed me to be *present*.

So, I showed up. Even when I was tired. Even when I was broke. Even when I felt like an imposter trying to teach about leadership when I was still learning how to lead myself.

But here's what I learned: leadership isn't about having all the answers it's about showing up with all your truth.

The more I gave, the more I healed. Every workshop, every school visit, every story I shared it was therapy. Not just for them. For me.

Slowly, I started to rebuild not just a life, but an identity. I wasn't just Terrance the street dude. I wasn't just Terrance the speaker. I was becoming Terrance the *healer.* The *builder.* The *leader. The Stepping Stone.*

And that's the real hustle.
Not chasing money. Not chasing clout.
Chasing *impact.*

Chapter Eleven Notes:

Quote: "Healing isn't a destination, it's a discipline."

Lesson: You don't have to be perfect to lead—you just have to be honest.

Leadership Takeaway: The most powerful leaders are those who lead while still learning.

Reflection Prompt: What part of your story could help heal someone else if you had the courage to share it?

CHAPTER
12

WHEN IT ALL CONNECTED

T he moment it all connected wasn't at a conference. It wasn't in a boardroom or a headline. It was in a classroom on the east side, with flickering lights, cracked tile floors, and kids who'd already been counted out.

I was doing a session with about 20 students in San Bernardino County Superintendent of Schools, most of them barely listening. A few slouched in their chairs, others half-heartedly scrolling on their phones. You could feel the "why-should-I-care" energy thick in the air.

I stood in front of them, paused for a moment, and said, "I used to think I wasn't going to make it past 21. Now I help kids like you find the kind of strength I had to build from pain."

One of them young brother in a hoodie, face cold as concrete leaned forward and asked, "What makes you think we even *can* change?"

I looked at him for a second, then said, "Because I already see who you really are. You're not lost you're *unseen*. I know that feeling. I was you."

That room got quiet. Real quiet. Something shifted. That kid who challenged me? He didn't walk out that day. He stayed after. Asked questions. Told me about his pops doing time. Told me about trying not to follow that same road but not knowing what else there was.

That was the moment.

Not because he changed that day. But because *I did.*

That's when I realized this wasn't about a nonprofit. It wasn't about speaking gigs. It was about *connection*. About one heart reaching another. And from that connection? Real transformation could happen.

From that day forward, I didn't just see Young Visionaries as an organization I saw it as a lifeline. A movement. A chance to change the temperature of a room just by walking in with purpose.

A few weeks later, the phone rang. One of my early funders called. Said they'd seen our work. Said the school district was talking. Said *something's happening.*

We got invited to speak at a city event. They gave us five minutes. I told the story of that classroom, of that kid, and what happens when we meet youth not with judgment, but with belief.

That five minutes turned into funding. That funding turned into space. That space turned into *impact.*

And just like that, it all connected.

Not because I figured it out. But because I never gave up on the belief that people, no matter how broken, can be restored and that restoration ripples.

Chapter Twelve Notes:

Quote: "The power to change the world starts with the courage to change one moment."

Lesson: The smallest breakthroughs can be the biggest signs you're on the right path.

Leadership Takeaway: True leadership is when your story gives someone else the strength to begin writing theirs.

Reflection Prompt: Who needs your story right now and are you willing to show up for that moment?

CHAPTER
13

THE COST OF CLARITY

W hen everything starts coming together, people think the hard part is over. But what they don't see is the weight that comes with clarity. Once you know your purpose, you can't go back to pretending you don't. There's no more comfort in the chaos. No more peace in the distractions.

Clarity is a gift but it's also a burden.

When Young Visionaries started growing, so did the pressure. The phone rang more. The rooms got bigger. The impact got deeper. But behind the scenes, I was still learning how to carry it all. I was still wrestling with the same question that haunted me since the beginning:

"Am I really enough for this?"

See, people love a redemption story but they don't always want the redeemed to lead. I'd walk into rooms with degrees hanging on walls and titles stitched into suits. I had none of that. What I had was pain.

Experience. Fire. But in those rooms, it often felt like I had to prove I deserved to be there just to breathe.

Some folks smiled in my face and whispered behind my back. Others straight up told me, "This isn't your lane."

But I knew what I carried. I knew that lived experience can't be taught in a classroom. I had survived systems that others only studied.

Still, there were nights I felt it heavy. The loneliness. The second-guessing. The expectations. I was leading a movement but I was still learning how to love myself without needing applause.

Still learning how to forgive the man I used to be, while growing into the man I was becoming.

Then came a moment I'll never forget. I was asked to speak at a youth leadership summit. Hundreds of students. Educators. Politicians. When I stepped on stage, I could feel the doubt in the room.

But I told my story.

Raw. Unfiltered. Honest.

And when I finished, there wasn't just applause. There were *tears*. Kids lined up to talk to me. One girl said, "That was the first time I felt like someone saw me."

That's when I realized clarity wasn't about comfort. It was about calling. And calling will always cost you something.

Sometimes it costs your ego. Sometimes your sleep. Sometimes your old friendships. But it always demands *all* of you.

And for the first time in my life, I was ready to give it.

Chapter Thirteen Notes:

Quote: "Purpose will break you open before it builds you up."

Lesson: The clearer your vision, the more courage it takes to carry it.

Leadership Takeaway: Real leaders don't just rise they wrestle.

Reflection Prompt: What has your purpose cost you so far and is it worth paying more to keep going?

CHAPTER

14

THE FIRE THAT DOESN'T
BURN OUT

———————————

You ever feel like you're running on fumes, but the fire inside just won't let you stop? That was me. After years of grind, of building this thing from nothing but faith and hustle, there were moments when I was flat-out exhausted. Mentally, physically, spiritually. But the mission kept pulling me back.

By this point, Young Visionaries was gaining momentum. Schools were calling. Cities were asking. Lives were being changed. But with more visibility came more pressure more expectations. I was being invited into rooms I never imagined I'd sit in. But behind the polished panels and smiling photo ops, I was still fighting the ghosts of who I used to be.

There were nights I'd go home from an event, take off the button-up, and sit in silence. The crowd may have clapped, the students may have nodded, but inside, I was questioning if I was really built for this long-term. Could I really carry the weight of this work for years to come? Could I stay healed while helping others heal?

That's when I realized something crucial: this work doesn't *save* you. It *reveals* you. And if you don't keep tending to your own fire, even purpose can burn you out.

So, I started doing something that felt foreign at first I poured back into *me.*

I prayed more. Sat still more. I started therapy. I journaled like my life depended on it because in many ways, it did. I reconnected with my kids. Started rebuilding relationships I had once sacrificed in the name of the mission. Because impact is meaningless if you're emotionally bankrupt.

The fire never died. But now, it burned *smarter.*

I stopped trying to prove myself to people who would never understand the trenches I came from. I stopped showing up to every opportunity just to be seen. Instead, I focused on being *effective.*

And in that season of deepening, of personal rebuilding, something shifted in me.

I no longer feared the work I welcomed it.

Because I knew that when I showed up, I wasn't just speaking from experience. I was speaking from *evidence.*

I had been the kid in the cell.

The man on the run.

The visionary with no budget.

And now, I was the proof that you can go from broken to builder.

From buried to blooming.

That fire? It wasn't burning me out anymore.

It was lighting the way for everyone still walking in the dark.

Chapter Fourteen Notes:

Quote: "The fire within you isn't meant to consume you it's meant to guide others."

Lesson: You don't have to burn out to shine. Protect your peace while pursuing your purpose.

Leadership Takeaway: Sustainable leadership starts with self-awareness and rest.

Reflection Prompt: How are you tending to the fire inside you so it fuels you instead of consuming you?

CHAPTER

15

THE MIRROR AND THE MIC

There comes a moment in your journey where the past, present, and future all collide and the only thing left is the mirror. No stage. No audience. No praise. Just you, your truth, and the reflection asking, "Who are you really?"

I had stood in front of crowds. I had helped kids find their footing. I had watched former gang members turn into community builders. But I hadn't fully turned the mic on myself. I hadn't faced the deepest parts of me. The parts that still held shame. The parts that still whispered, "You're just pretending."

It happened during a leadership retreat. I wasn't speaking. I was attending. Sitting in the back, playing it low-key. The facilitator said, "Turn to the person next to you and tell them the truth you've never said out loud."

I froze. All the speeches I had given. All the panels I'd sat on. None of it prepared me for that.

The truth I'd never said out loud?

"I'm afraid I'll always be defined by who I was not who I am."

It hit me hard. Because as much as I had grown, there was still a version of me locked in survival mode. And that version needed to be heard not just buried.

After that moment, I started speaking differently. Not louder. Not smoother. Just *truer.*

I shared my scars, not just my success. I talked about the guilt I still carried. The healing I was still doing. The ways I was learning how to be a better father, a better son, a better man.

And that's when I noticed something powerful.

The more real I became, the more others felt safe to be real too.

The mic wasn't just a tool for education it was a mirror for liberation. It helped others see themselves not through judgment, but through possibility.

Young Visionaries wasn't just about mentoring kids anymore. It was about mentoring *men.* About healing cycles. About breaking generational patterns.

I began creating space for other formerly incarcerated brothers to speak. To lead. To reclaim their voice. Because the truth is, when one of us rises with honesty, it creates a bridge for others to walk across.

And bridges matter more than barriers.

We'd sit in circles with young people and say, "We've been where you are. And you don't have to stay there." And when they saw that reflection in us, when they heard that truth in our voices they believed.

The mirror helped me find myself.
The mic helped me free others.
And together, they built a legacy that no lie could erase.

Chapter 15 Notes:

Quote: "Your voice becomes powerful the moment it stops hiding your truth."

Lesson: You can't lead others to healing if you haven't looked into your own wounds.

Leadership Takeaway: Vulnerability isn't weakness it's access.

Reflection Prompt: What truth are you holding back that could be the key to someone else's freedom?

PART IV: THE WORK NEVER STOPS

_____

HEALING IN PUBLIC

Healing is messy. It's not a straight line. It's not always quiet. And when your life's been as loud and public as mine healing becomes something, you do in front of people who still see you as who you used to be.

When I first started opening up more in my talks when I started telling the deeper truths, the broken parts I noticed a shift. Some people leaned in. Others backed away. But either way, they were watching.

There's something raw about trying to heal out loud while still carrying the scars. Not old ones the fresh ones. The kind that still sting when you speak on them. And the reality is, I wasn't just healing from the past. I was healing from the pressure of the *present.*

See, when you're a leader from the streets, the hood doesn't give you grace. They give you expectations. "Be tough." "Don't cry." "Stay ten toes." But what if you're just trying to stay human?

There were days I was encouraging others while I was falling apart. Nights I went home from events where I'd helped kids avoid violence but couldn't sleep because I still carried guilt from my own past. And in those moments, I had to remind myself: healing isn't a destination, it's a rhythm.

So, I started being even more transparent.

I'd tell the kids, "Yes, I've changed. But I still get triggered."

I'd tell the men in my circle, "Yes, I lead. But I also cry. I also doubt. I also struggle."

And the wild part? That honesty didn't push people away. It pulled them in. Because real recognizes *real healing.*

I watched grown men, ex-gangsters, dudes with rap sheets longer than their arms open up about their pain, their parenting fears, their depression. And I'd sit there in awe, thinking: *This is what the world needs to see.*

Not just success stories. Not just highlight reels. But the middle of the mess. The work. The fight to keep showing up.

That's what Chapter 16 of my journey is: the choice to heal in front of the same people I once had to survive in front of.

Because healing in private is strength. But healing in public? That's legacy.

Chapter Sixteen Notes:

Quote: "Healing in front of others gives them permission to begin their own."

Lesson: The bravest thing you can do is grow even when people are watching.

Leadership Takeaway: True leadership isn't about having it all together it's about moving forward, even when you're still piecing yourself back together.

Reflection Prompt: Who needs to see your healing journey not your highlight reel?

THE ONES WE LOSE, THE ONES WE REACH

Every win we stack in this work comes with a shadow the memory of the ones we couldn't save. And if I'm being real, some nights, it's those losses that echo the loudest.

You never forget the funerals. The candles on the sidewalk. The phone calls that start with, "Did you hear about..."

Sometimes it's a kid you just spoke to last week. Told him to keep his head up. Told him he had options. Sometimes he believed it. But sometimes, the streets pulled harder than hope.

I remember one kid we'll call him Marcus. Bright. Angry. Funny as hell. Had bars, too. Used to freestyle while the other boys clowned around. I saw the light in him. I poured into him every chance I got. One night he didn't come to the program. Next day, I found out he got shot two blocks from where we used to meet.

That pain hit different.

Because when you're doing this kind of work, your heart stretches. It makes space for every kid who reminds you of who you were. And when you lose one, it feels like a piece of your soul gets buried too.

But here's the truth: you can't stay buried. Because the ones you *do* reach? They still need you to stand. To show up. To fight.

For every Marcus, there was a Jamal who graduated. A Tasha who opened her own salon. A Luis who came back to mentor after doing a bid.

These wins? They keep me going.

But it's more than just survival stories. It's about creating a culture of *belonging*. A place where young people feel seen, heard, and protected. Because that's what most of them are fighting for a space to be themselves without having to prove how tough they are.

We throw around phrases like "at-risk youth." But risk ain't just about behavior it's about what's missing. Love. Safety. Opportunity. And when we restore that, we shift everything.

That's why I keep showing up. Even when it hurts.

Because the work is sacred. And the lives we save those are the *real receipts* of this calling.

So, to every young one I've lost you're not forgotten. And to every young one still trying I'm not done.

Chapter Seventeen Notes:

Quote: "We carry the pain of who we lost but we keep fighting for who's still here."

Lesson: Grief doesn't mean you stop it means you carry more carefully.

Leadership Takeaway: Leaders mourn, but they also *move*. Because purpose must continue, even though the tears.

Reflection Prompt: Who are you still fighting for, even when it hurts and what does that say about your calling?

CHAPTER

18

LEGACY IN MOTION

There's a moment when the grind becomes more than just work it becomes a legacy. Not the kind etched in stone or printed on plaques. I'm talking about the legacy that lives in people. In changed lives. In futures re-routed. In stories rewritten.

I used to think legacy was something you earned *after* you died. Now I know it's what you *build while you live.* Every time I speak, every time I mentor, every kid who calls me "OG" with respect in their voice that's legacy in motion.

There was a young man named Isaiah. He came into the program with fire in his eyes and a chip on his shoulder the size of the streets he was running from. First day, he barely spoke. Second day, he challenged everything I said. Third day, he asked if I ever thought about giving up.

I told him, "Every day. But I never let that thought make the decision for me."

That hit him different.

Two years later, Isaiah stood next to me on a stage. He shared his story to a room full of city leaders. No script. No filter. Just truth. And when he finished, people stood and clapped not because he was polished, but because he was *real.*

That's when I knew: my legacy wasn't just in what I built it was in who I *built up.*

The streets used to write our stories in blood. In chalk outlines and closed caskets. But now? We write our stories in light. In leadership. In love.

Young Visionaries isn't just a program anymore. It's a movement. It's a declaration that no matter where you come from, you can rise. You can lead. You can *live.*

And for me? I'm not done yet. The work doesn't stop because you get a little recognition. If anything, it pushes you to go harder.

Legacy is loud. But it's also quiet. It's found in a hug. In a "thank you" whispered after everyone leaves. In a text that says, "I didn't do it. I made it home."

That's the work. That's the reward.

And that's what keeps me moving in every room full of vultures because I know I'm walking with purpose.

Chapter Eighteen Notes:

Quote: "Legacy isn't what you leave behind it's what you pour into others while you're still here."

Lesson: The most lasting impact isn't made in headlines, but in hearts.

Leadership Takeaway: True leaders create leaders not followers.

Reflection Prompt: What kind of legacy are you building through your daily actions and who's being shaped by it?

THE ROOM FULL OF VULTURES

I used to walk into rooms and feel like prey. Eyes watching. Judging. Doubting. Measuring me by my worst mistakes, never my best intentions. But something shifted along the way not just in how they saw me, but in how I saw *myself.*

That's when I learned: you can't control the vultures, but you can control how you move.

And when you walk with purpose, with truth, with vision they stop circling. They start listening.

Every room I walk into now carries that weight. I know who's watching. I know what they expect. Some wait for me to slip. Others want to see if I'll rise. Either way, I don't walk in for *them.* I walk in for the ones who need to see what resilience looks like in real time.

I've stood in courtrooms and classrooms. City halls and community centers. I've been on stages with politicians and behind closed doors with young brothers who just caught their first case. And in every room, I bring the same truth: *I'm still here. Still healing. Still building.*

Some rooms feel like traps. Others feel like platforms. But all of them? They're opportunities. Not just to speak but to shift. To change the temperature. To let people know you can come from the bottom and still lead with dignity.

Sometimes leadership means speaking boldly. Other times, it means standing in silence and letting your presence do the talking.

I've learned to walk tall in rooms that were never built for me. Because when you carry the stories of the forgotten, you don't need to raise your voice, you *are* the message.

So, when I say, "How to move in a room full of vultures," I'm not just talking about survival. I'm talking about transformation.

How to walk with your head high even when they whisper. How to keep your soul intact when the system tried to steal it. How to stand in your story without shame because every scar is proof you made it through.

This isn't about impressing anyone. It's about empowering everyone.

And if I can do that even in the darkest, coldest, most hostile rooms then maybe the next young brother or sister watching will know they can too.

Because the vultures only win when you stop flying.

Chapter Nineteen Notes:

Quote: "The room doesn't define you how you move in it does."

Lesson: Respect isn't demanded it's embodied.

Leadership Takeaway: The most powerful leaders don't just survive in the room they change the atmosphere.

Reflection Prompt: What space have you been shrinking in and how would it feel to walk in with your full truth?

CHAPTER

20

FULL CIRCLE

It took me a long time to realize that redemption isn't a destination. It's a decision you make every single day. To wake up. To keep going. To stay committed to healing, to growing, to leading even when you're tired, doubted, or dismissed.

Standing here now, looking at what Young Visionaries has become, looking at the men and women we've reached, the lives we've helped redirect, I feel two things: gratitude and fire. Gratitude for every step it took to get here. Fire because the work ain't done.

There's no bow on this story. No fairy tale ending. The community still hurts. The streets are still calling some of our youth louder than hope is. But now? We've got louder voices speaking back. We've got soldiers of peace showing up on front lines of despair with open arms instead of closed fists.

Every time I get up to speak, I'm reminded of the boy I used to be the one who didn't think he'd make it to twenty-one. And now, I get to speak life into kids who don't think they'll make it either. That's full circle.

I've walked out of cells. I've walked through courts. I've walked into schools. I've walked into city halls and state capital buildings. And everywhere I go I bring that same kid with me. Not in shame, but in honor. Because he survived. Because *I* survived.

And now, I lead.

Not just to be seen. Not just to prove a point. But because every room I enter, I know there's a young person watching, wondering if there's another way.

There is.

You don't have to move with fear. You don't have to move with hate. You don't have to move for validation.

You can move with purpose. You can move with love. You can move with vision.

And yes, you can move in a room full of vultures.

Because when you walk in truth, the vultures starve.

This book is not about me. It's about all of us who've ever been counted out, locked up, written off, or told we'd never rise. Look at us now.

This is your invitation. To keep going. To keep leading. To keep healing.

To move fully, fearlessly, and free.

Chapter Twenty Notes:

Quote: "Redemption is not a moment, it's a movement."

Lesson: Your story is still being written and every chapter matters.

Leadership Takeaway: The most impactful leaders never forget where they came from, they just refuse to stay there.

Reflection Prompt: What legacy will you choose to live today and who will it inspire tomorrow?

PHOTO GALLERY

TERRANCE STONE CYA
PHOTO

Terrance Stone California Youth Authority 17 Years Old

GLADIATOR SCHOOL 1988
(CYA)

Terrance Stone far right California Youth Authority circa 1988

CALIFORNIA STATE PRISON

Terrance Stone California State Prison 24 Years Old circa 1994

Terrance Stone 1996

TERRANCE STONE 1996

Terrance Stone California State Prison

circa1993

TERRANCE STONE
CALIFORNIA STATE PRISON
CIRCA1993

———————————

TERRANCE STONE NOMINATED COMMUNITY ICON IN 2024

Terrance Stone Nominated Community Icon in 2024 from JP Morgan Chase Bank

TERRANCE STONE ON THE COVER OF INLAND SCENE

Terrance Stone on the Cover of

Inland Scene Magazine 2017

Inland Scene

Terrance Stone Certified Gang Specialist

TERRANCE STONE
CERTIFIED GANG
SPECIALIST

TERRANCE STONE TV
INTERVIEW 2020

———————————————

STATE OF CALIFORNIA MAN OF THE YEAR 2022

————————————

STATE CAPITOL
P.O. BOX 942849
SACRAMENTO, CA 94249-0047
(916) 319-2047
FAX (916) 319-2147

DISTRICT OFFICE
290 NORTH D STREET, SUITE 903
SAN BERNARDINO, CA 92401
(909) 381-3238
FAX (909) 885-8589

E-MAIL
Assemblymember.Reyes@assembly.ca.gov

Assembly
California Legislature

ELOISE GÓMEZ REYES
MAJORITY LEADER
ASSEMBLYMEMBER, FORTY-SEVENTH DISTRICT

COMMITTEES
AGING AND LONG-TERM CARE
BUDGET
JUDICIARY
LABOR AND EMPLOYMENT
UTILITIES AND ENERGY

BUDGET SUBCOMMITTEE NO. 2 ON
EDUCATION FINANCE

LEGISLATIVE ETHICS

April 7, 2022

RE: Assembly District 47 Man of the Year Finalist

Dear Mr. Stone:

Congratulations! You were selected as a finalist for the 47th Assembly District Man of the Year Award due to your unwavering dedication to uplifting and supporting the community around you. This honor recognizes men who have made a significant contribution in the 47th Assembly District.

Please confirm your selection by sending a brief biography (200 words) and high-resolution photo directly to Prince Ogidikpe at Prince.Ogidikpe@asm.ca.gov by Wednesday, April 13,

I cordially invite you to celebrate your nomination on Thursday, April 21, 2022, 2:00 pm – 4:00 pm. The will be held virtually on zoom.

Please RSVP by Friday, April 15th directly to Prince Ogidikpe at (909) 381-3238 or Prince.Ogidikpe@asm.ca.gov.

We look forward to celebrating with you. Again, congratulations on your selection!

Sincerely,

ELOISE GÓMEZ REYES
Majority Leader, 47th District

Terrance Stone, Young Visionaries Leadership Academy help hundreds of San Bernardino County students

Terrance Stone sits in his office in the warehouse area of San Bernardino. He has received numerous awards in

Sun Newspaper

TERRANCE STONE
NEWSPAPER ARTICLE 2021

TERRANCE STONE RUNNING
FOR PUBLIC OFFICE 2020

PRESIDENTS MEDAL FROM CAL STATE SAN BERNARDINO

October 12, 2023

Mr. Terrance L. Stone

Dear Mr. Stone: *Terrance*

I am writing to inform you that you have been selected to receive the President's Medal on behalf of California State University, San Bernardino in recognition of your accomplishments as founder and CEO of Young Visionaries Youth Leadership Academy, as president of Terrance Stone School and Community Consulting, as a nationally and state-certified gang specialist, author, philanthropist, and as an award-winning advocate for young lives.

The President's Medal is awarded in recognition of an individual's extraordinary service. This exclusive award is the highest honor that California State University, San Bernardino will bestow upon a non-graduate of the university.

If you accept this distinction, I will have the pleasure of presenting you with the President's Medal at the President's Dinner, which will be held on Thursday, November 30, 2023, from 5:30 p.m. to 8:30 p.m., at the Mission Inn in Riverside. I will host you and your guest that evening.

If you have any questions, Robert Nava, Vice President for University Advancement, will provide you with additional information and will confirm your attendance.

Thank you for considering this honor and I look forward to seeing you on November 30.

Sincerely,

Tomás D. Morales
President

cc: Robert Nava, Vice President, University Advancement

909.537.5002 · fax: 909.537.5901 · www.csusb.edu/president
5500 UNIVERSITY PARKWAY, SAN BERNARDINO, CA 92407-2393

The California State University · Bakersfield · Channel Islands · Chico · Dominguez Hills · East Bay · Fresno · Fullerton · Humboldt · Long Beach · Los Angeles
Maritime Academy · Monterey Bay · Northridge · Pomona · Sacramento · San Bernardino · San Diego · San Francisco · San Jose · San Luis Obispo · San Marcos · Sonoma · Stanislaus

Author's Note

If you made it this far, I just want to say thank you. Thank you for letting me share my scars, my growth, my lessons and my love. Writing this wasn't easy. Reliving it wasn't comfortable. But I knew that someone, somewhere, needed to know it's possible to go from pain to purpose. If that's you keep moving. Keep building. Keep becoming.

You're not alone. We're in this together.

To the adults, leaders, mentors, and folks with resources: We can't save everybody, but we can *show up* for somebody. And if enough of us show up for *somebody*, we just might save *everybody*.

This isn't just my story, it's the story of thousands of kids, communities, and families trying to make it, to matter, and to move forward.

And we're not done yet. That's why I'm asking you, from the heart to invest in the movement. Support the mission. **Be a part of the miracle.**

Visit www.yvyla-ie.org and donate whatever you can. Every dollar helps us put mentors in schools, jobs in hands, food on tables, backpacks on kids, and hope into hearts. Every donation is a seed that grows a safer, stronger, more powerful tomorrow.

We've already impacted over 200,000 youth—and we're just getting started.

Young Visionaries is bigger than one man, one story, or one organization.

It's a movement.

It's every kid that didn't give up. Every parent who kept praying. Every teacher who didn't quit. Every street soldier who decided to put the gun down and pick purpose up.
So, here's the truth:

You were never too broken to be restored. You were never too lost to be found. And you were never too far gone to come back and *build something legendary.*

Because if someone like me can find their way, then *so can you.*

The world may try to count you out. But I promise, if you just keep showing up—*you'll count for something much greater.*

Keep pushing. Keep praying. And never forget—**your crown is still waiting.**

— *Dr. Terrance L. Stone*

Leadership Toolkit: 20 Lessons to Move with Power

This section is for the ones ready to lead. Whether you're fresh out, still stuck, or starting over these tools are yours.

1. **Know your story. Own your scars.**

   Don't let shame silence you. Your past is your power.

2. **Don't just survive—strategize.**

   Plan. Move with intention. Think long-term.

3. **Presence over posture.**

   You don't have to be loud to be felt. Be solid.

4. **Stay teachable.**

   You can't lead if you can't learn.

5. **Build what you didn't have.**

   Create the resource, the mentor, the safe space you needed.

6. **Read everything.**

   Leaders are readers. Knowledge keeps you sharp.

7. **Speak life.**

   Your words have weight. Use them to uplift, not destroy.

8. **Be consistent.**

   People trust what they see you do over and over.

9. **Protect your peace.**

   Not every battle is worth fighting.

10. **Lead from where you are.**

    You don't need a title to lead—just vision and action.

11. **Keep it 100.**

    Integrity is non-negotiable. Say what you mean. Mean what you say.

12. **Pass the mic.**

    Make room for others to shine. That's real power.

13. **Stay rooted.**

    Don't forget where you came from—but don't let it limit where you're going.

14. **Elevate the room.**

    Bring wisdom, not ego. Light, not heat.

15. **Rest is resistance.**
    Take care of your mental, emotional, and physical health.
16. **Be the example.**
    Don't just talk about it. Live it.
17. **Reinvest.**
    Pour back into the people and places that raised you.
18. **Lead like someone's watching.**
    Because they are. Always.
19. **Stay dangerous—in the right way.**
    Be so focused, so disciplined, so purpose-driven—it's threatening.
20. **Lead with love.**
    Nothing heals, builds, or transforms like love. Lead from that place and you'll always win.

Use these tools however you need. Tape them to your mirror. Share them with your crew. Teach them in your classroom. Tattoo them on your soul.

Just don't sit on your leadership.

Move with it.

Companion Workbook

DEALING WITH TRAUMA

HOW TO MOVE IN
A ROOM
FULL OF
VULTURES

DR. TERRANCE L. STONE

Introduction to the Workbook

This workbook is designed to help you reflect, process, and activate the lessons found in *How to Move in a Room Full of Vultures*. Each chapter section includes writing prompts, journaling space, and exercises to help you apply the book's wisdom to your own life and leadership.

Whether you're a youth navigating tough streets, a mentor trying to guide others, or someone rebuilding your life from the ground up—this space is yours.
Use it to:

- Reflect on your own pain, progress, and purpose
- Capture visions for the future
- Build a blueprint for leadership and legacy

Remember: you don't have to have it all together. You just have to keep showing up.

Terrance Stone Bio

Dr. Terrance L. Stone is an inspirational leader who has dedicated his life to empowering young people and helping them discover their true purpose. In 2001 he founded and is CEO of **Young Visionaries Youth Leadership Academy**, President of **Terrance Stone School and Community Consulting**, and the President of The **Southern California Black Chamber of Commerce High Desert Chapter**.

With over 200,000 at-risk youth reached, Mr. Stone is a nationally and state-certified gang intervention and prevention specialist who has helped diffuse conflicts between gangs and set up a workforce development program that provides training and jobs for young people. He and his male career members have also started a men mob, which has expanded to greet students on over 50 campuses in California, that encourages and changes the attitudes of many young people towards education.

Dr. Stone's advocacy work has been recognized nationally and internationally, including several awards such as the West Coast Hip Hop Community Influencer Award in 2023 and the Unforgettable Hearts Award in 2023.

As an author of the book **"How to Move in a Room Full of Vultures,"** he encourages young people to realize their potential and understand that they have everything they need to succeed. Dr. Stone is also an avid philanthropist, providing food baskets for thousands of families during Thanksgiving and toys and food baskets during Christmas.

His vast professional affiliations speak to his involvement in his community, paving the way for him to establish himself as a leader and a role model. Mr. Stone has also been featured in various publications, including the New York Times and MSNBC, as well as in television and radio interviews.

Professional Affiliations To Date (2025):

- State and National Certified Gang Intervention and Prevention Specialist
- Past San Bernardino County District Attorney Office Community Commission Member
- San Bernardino City Chief of Police African American Advisory Committee
- San Bernardino County Probation JJCC Executive Sub Committee on DJJ
- San Bernardino County Sheriffs Information Exchange Committee
- San Bernardino County Superior Courts Gang Consultant
- San Bernardino County Community Vital Signs Board Member
- San Bernardino Countywide Gangs and Drugs Taskforce Board Member
- Excelsior Charter School Board Member for San Bernardino & Riverside Counties
- Cooperative Economic Empowerment Movement (CEEM) Board Member
- Southern California Black Chamber of Commerce – High Desert Chapter President
- Maggie's Kids Foundation Board Member
- San Bernardino County Equity Element Committee (Racism is a Public Health Crises)
- San Bernardino County Workforce Development Board Special Populations Committee
- Past City of Victorville Community Services Advisory Committee Commissioner
- Tri State Community Health Care Board Member
- Terrance Stone School and Community Consulting LLC

- Young Visionaries President/CEO

Sincere efforts have resulted in Dr. Stone receiving hundreds of awards to date:

- 2024 JPMorgan Chase Community Icon Award
- 2024 The Deborah Robertson Foundation's Hardy Brown Sr. Exemplary Service Award
- 2024 IEHP Inspire Award
- 2023 Inland Empire Choice Lifetime Achievement Award
- 2023 Cal State San Bernardino Presidents Medal
- 2023 Southern California Black Chamber Presidential Award of Excellence
- 2023 Bishop Ron Allen Award-California Association of Code Enforcement Officers
- 2023 Official West Coast Hip Hop Community Influencer Award
- 2023 BFSSA Cal State San Bernardino The Village Award
- 2023 10th Annual Unforgettable Hearts Award
- 2022 Non Profit of the Year
- 2022 Children Deserve Success Award from SBCSS
- 2020 Martin Luther King Community Service Award
- 2019 Distinguished Service in Civic and Community Service Award
- 2018 Tom Bradley Community Service & Distinguished Citizen Award
- 2018 Todays Leadership Spark Creating Leaders Through Youth Enrichment Award
- 2018 DVL Icon Award
- 2017 Boy Scouts of America Whitney M. Young Jr. Service Award
- 2016 Dignity Health Community Service Award
- 2015 Model of Excellence Award
- 2014 Beacon of Light Award
- 2014 Shine the Light On Child Abuse Award
- 2013 Best of the Best for Inland Empire Business

- 2013 Spirit of the Entrepreneur Award Winner for Social Entrepreneur
- 2013 Inland Empire Unit of National Association of Social Workers Public Citizen of Year Award
- 2012 Trail Blazer Award
- 2012 Senator Man of the Year Award
- 2012 Unforgettable Hearts Award ~
- 2011 Gertude Whetzel Award
- 2011 Man of Valor
- 2010 Community Pillar Award for Fairness
- 2010 Executive of the Year Award
- 2010 Time for Change Pioneer Award
- 2010 San Bernardino County Education Medal of Honor Award
- 2010 CAHPERD Emmett Ashford Community Spirit Award
- 2008 Juvenile Justice & Delinquency Prevention Commission San Bernardino County
- 2008 Unsung Hero Award
- 2008 Black Rose Award
- 2008 Social Lites Community Service Award
- 2007 Amanda Guruge Lifetime Commitment Award
- 2007 Man of Valor Award Jubilee House of Praise
- 2007 Molina Healthcare of California Community Champion Award
- 2007 People's Choice Inc "Leaders of Youth Award" Recipient
- 2006 Excellence Award Recipient
- 2006 Citizens of Achievement Award Recipient
- 2006 Youth Outreach Award Recipient
- 2005 "Inspiration to Youth" Good Samaritan Award Recipient
- 2005 Social Action Trailblazers Award Recipient

Session 1:

Reflection Prompt:

- What's one early childhood experience that shaped how you see yourself today?
- Who were your first role models—good or bad—and what did they teach you?

Journaling Space: *Use this page to write about the moment you realized the world wasn't safe—but that you had to survive it anyway.*

Leadership Activation: Write down one leadership quality you wish you saw growing up—and commit to becoming that for someone else.

_____
_____
_____
_____
_____
_____
_____
_____
_____
_____
_____
_____
_____
_____

Session 2:

Reflection Prompt:

- What relationships shaped your understanding of brotherhood or loyalty?
- How did family dynamics (biological or chosen) shape who you became?

Journaling Space: *Who's someone who challenged you and helped you grow—even through conflict?*

Leadership Activation: How can you create unity within your circle instead of chaos? List 3 ways.

_____

_____

_____

_____

_____

_____

_____

_____

_____

_____

_____

_____

_____

_____

_____

_____

_____

_____

_____

Session 3:

Reflection Prompt:

- Have you ever chased fast success and felt the consequences later?
- What "freedom" did the streets offer you—and what did it cost?

Journaling Space: *Describe a moment when you realized the hustle had a price.*

Leadership Activation: What long-term goals can you start working on today that will outlast temporary wins?

_____
_____
_____
_____
_____
_____
_____
_____
_____
_____
_____
_____
_____
_____
_____
_____
_____

Session 4:

Reflection Prompt:
- What experiences taught you how to protect yourself mentally and emotionally?
- Have you ever had to prove yourself in a way that didn't align with your values?

Journaling Space: *Write about a time you were underestimated and how you responded.*

Leadership Activation: Name one way you can lead through peace instead of fear this week.

_____

_____

_____

_____

_____

_____

_____

_____

_____

_____

_____

_____

_____

_____

_____

Session 5:

Reflection Prompt:

· What patterns or habits have been the hardest to walk away from?
· What does the "old you" still try to call you back to?

Journaling Space: *Write about a turning point where you wanted change but kept slipping back.*

Leadership Activation: What does the future version of you look like? Describe them in detail.

Session 6:

Reflection Prompt:

- What has it cost you to pretend everything was fine when it wasn't?
- What fills you up when you're running low?

Journaling Space: *Describe what "running on fumes" looks like in your life.*

Leadership Activation: List 5 healthy ways to recharge when life gets overwhelming.

_____

_____

_____

_____

_____

_____

_____

_____

_____

_____

_____

_____

_____

_____

_____

_____

_____

_____

Session 7:

Reflection Prompt:
- How do you respond to setbacks? With shame or strategy?
- Who supports you even when you fall off?

Journaling Space: *Write about a time you slipped—and what you learned from it.*

Leadership Activation: Set a "bounce-back" plan. What will you do the next time you slip?

_____
_____
_____
_____
_____
_____
_____
_____
_____
_____
_____
_____
_____
_____
_____
_____
_____

Session 8:

Reflection Prompt:

· Have you ever felt forced to choose survival over your dreams?
· What "setups" have threatened your progress?

Journaling Space: *Write about a decision you made out of pressure, not purpose.*

Leadership Activation: Create a plan for how you'll choose purpose over pressure next time.

_____
_____
_____
_____
_____
_____
_____
_____
_____
_____
_____
_____
_____
_____
_____
_____
_____
_____

DR. TERRANCE STONE

Session 9:

Reflection Prompt:

- What have you been running from emotionally, mentally, or spiritually?
- What's one thing you're tired of hiding?

Journaling Space: *Reflect on a time when hiding felt easier than healing.*

Leadership Activation: Name one person you trust. What's one truth you could share with them?

_____
_____
_____
_____
_____
_____
_____
_____
_____
_____
_____
_____
_____
_____
_____
_____

Session 10:

Reflection **Prompt:**

· Who believed in you when you didn't believe in yourself?
· What responsibilities forced you to level up?

Journaling Space: *Write about a moment where someone saw your potential before you did.*

Leadership Activation: How can you recognize and call out greatness in someone else this week?

_____
_____
_____
_____
_____
_____
_____
_____
_____
_____
_____
_____
_____
_____
_____
_____
_____
_____

Session 11:

Reflection Prompt:

- What's one dream you've buried but never stopped thinking about?
- What's holding you back from chasing it now?

Journaling Space: *Describe the version of your life where you followed your dream.*

Leadership Activation: List 3 small steps you can take toward that dream this month.

_____

_____

_____

_____

_____

_____

_____

_____

_____

_____

_____

_____

_____

_____

_____

_____

_____

_____

_____

Session 12:

Reflection Prompt:

· What's something you built from nothing?
· What sacrifices did it take to get here?

Journaling Space: *Reflect on the hustle it took to build something real.*

Leadership Activation: Who or what are you building for? Write your "why" statement.

_____
_____
_____
_____
_____
_____
_____
_____
_____
_____
_____
_____
_____
_____
_____
_____
_____
_____

Session 13:

Reflection Prompt:
- What's one survival habit you've outgrown?
- What's one strategic habit you're building?

Journaling Space: *Write about your transition from reacting to planning.*

Leadership Activation: Draft a one-year vision plan with 3 goals and action steps.

_____
_____
_____
_____
_____
_____
_____
_____
_____
_____
_____
_____
_____
_____
_____
_____
_____
_____
_____

Session 14:

Reflection Prompt:

- Who are you influencing right now whether you know it or not?
- What legacy do you want to leave?

Journaling Space: *Imagine what someone will say about you 10 years from now.*

Leadership Activation: List 3 ways you can pour into the next generation this year.

_____
_____
_____
_____
_____
_____
_____
_____
_____
_____
_____
_____
_____
_____
_____
_____
_____
_____

Session 15:

Reflection Prompt:

- How can your story be a platform to help others?
- What message do you carry that someone else needs to hear?

Journaling Space: *Write your "I made it through" story.*

Leadership Activation: Turn your pain into purpose: write a speech, a post, or a message to someone who's struggling now.

_____
_____
_____
_____
_____
_____
_____
_____
_____
_____
_____
_____
_____
_____
_____
_____
_____
_____
_____

Session 16:

Reflection Prompt:
· What does legacy mean to you?
· How do you want people to feel when they hear your name?

Journaling Space: *Describe your legacy in one paragraph. Be bold.*

Leadership Activation: Choose one habit you'll commit to daily that supports your legacy.

_____

_____

_____

_____

_____

_____

_____

_____

_____

_____

_____

_____

_____

_____

_____

_____

_____

Session 17:

Reflection Prompt:
- What makes your foundation solid?
- Who helped you get started, and how can you honor them?

Journaling Space: *Write about your journey—from where you started to where you are now.*

Leadership Activation: Create a "vision board" page here. Use drawings, words, photos, or affirmations that reflect where you're going.

_____

_____

_____

_____

_____

_____

_____

_____

_____

_____

_____

_____

_____

_____

_____

_____

_____

_____

_____

Bonus Section: Build Your Own Blueprint

Daily Check-In Prompts:

- What am I grateful for today?
- What challenge am I facing?
- What's one step I can take today toward growth?

_____
_____
_____
_____
_____
_____
_____
_____
_____
_____
_____
_____
_____
_____
_____
_____
_____
_____
_____
_____
_____

Affirmations Page:

- I am not my past—I am my purpose.
- I am worthy of peace, progress, and power.
- I lead with love, even when it's hard.

Vision Space:

L eave blank space here for artwork, drawings, or goal-mapping.

About the Author:

Dr. Terrance L. Stone knows what it means to walk through the fire and come out refined. A former gang member turned community leader; Terrance has dedicated his life to being the man he once needed. As the Founder and CEO of *Young Visionaries Youth Leadership Academy* and President of the Southern California Black Chamber of Commerce High Desert Chapter, he's helped guide over 200,000 at-promise youth toward brighter futures, using the pain of his past as fuel for his purpose.

Whether he's standing at the gates of a school in a suit, greeting kids with encouragement, or sitting with families after tragedy to help them heal, Terrance leads with heart, humility, and faith. His journey has taken him from the streets to stages across the country and the world, sharing a message of hope, accountability, and God-given potential.

Terrance isn't just building programs—he's building people. And through every story he shares, he reminds us all that redemption is real, leadership is learned, and purpose is always within reach.